Getting Started on
DJEMBE
with Michael Wimberly

HUDSON MUSIC®

Inside This Book

Getting Started on Djembe / by Michael Wimberly

Edited by Joe Bergamini

Book Design, Layout and Music Engraving by Rick Gratton

Photos by Andrew Lepley

Cover Design by Mike Hoff

Executive Producers: Paul Siegel and Rob Wallis

All musical examples and tracks written by Michael Wimberly

Used by permission

For information about the Hudson Music catalog of DVDs and print/audio products for musicians, please visit www.hudsonmusic.com.

The Author / Michael Wimberly

Michael Wimberly is a classically-trained percussionist and composer who holds a master's degree in music from Manhattan School of Music. But it is his study of African percussion that makes his compositions most unique and sets both audiences and critics on fire. Michael has defied categorization by mixing European textures, ancient African rhythms, and modern American music, creating a muse of sound that is as electrifying as it is multi-cultural.

Born and raised in Cleveland, Ohio, Michael discovered at an early age that he had a passion for music. Since then, he has recorded, performed and toured with jazz artists such as Charles Gayle, Jean Paul Bourelly, Steve Coleman's 5 Elements, David Murray Octet, and Teramasa Hino Quartet; world music artists Paul Winter Consort, John McDowell and Mamma Tongue; funk and R&B legends George Clinton and the Parliment Funkadelics, D'Angelo, Angie Stone, and Alyson Williams; and rock icons Vernon Reid, Henry Rollins, Blondie, and Mickey Hart. As a soloist, Michael has performed with Berlin's Rundfunk Symphony Orchestra, Vienna's Tonkuntsler Symphony Orchestra, International Regions Orchestra, and composed for the Yakima Chamber Orchestra in Yakima, Washington.

Michael's compositions appear in the repertoire of luminary dance companies Urban Bush Women, Joffrey Ballet, Alvin Ailey, Philadanco, Forces of Nature, Ailey II, Complexions, Ballet Noir, Alpha Omega, Purelements and The National Song and Dance Company of Mozambique.

As CEO of MW Productions Sound Design (a Michael Wimberly Entertainment Company), Michael has positioned his musical scores and sound designs in several New York City Off-Broadway theaters including The Public Theater, Cherry Lane Theater, The Women's Project, Ensemble Studio Theater, The Greenwich House Theater, The Harvey 651 @ BAM, and Lincoln Center Performing Arts Center. Regional theaters include The Cleveland Playhouse, Cleveland, OH; Cross Roads Theatre, New Brunswick NJ; Bates College, Portland MN; Syracuse University, Syracuse NY; The Kennedy Center, Washington DC; Columbia College, Chicago Il; Paramount Theater, Seattle WA; The Seasons, Yakima WA; and The Alliance Theatre in Atlanta GA.

Michael's work with young adults and children of all ages has positioned him to work as a teaching artist under the umbrella of the US Department of Education, Arts Connection, Cooke Academy, Ethical Cultural Fieldston School, KOSA International Drum Camp, Lehman College, the Museum for African Art, Borough of Manhattan Community College, Central Park Conservancy, and as music faculty with Bennington College, VT. Michael's passion for teaching music inspired him to create a percussionist showcase and clinic event called the Power of Drum held in New York City; Yakima, Washington; and Saô Miguel in the Azores, Portugal. Currently, Michael is President of the Michael Wimberly Cooperative - Together with Music, which is located on the island of Sao Miguel, Portugal.

Author's Introduction: I was introduced to the djembe and its family of drums while studying percussion at Baldwin Wallace College in Berea, Ohio. My friend from New York, Craig Brown, was majoring in classical organ at the school's conservatory. Craig was a straight-A student, a great musician, and he happened to have two djembes and a sangban (African bass drum) in his dorm room. On the weekends we would go to his room and play the drums for hours. Craig was very knowledgeable about djembe rhythms, African dance, and African culture in general. He taught us the songs and rhythms that he learned from the Chuck Davis Dance Company (which was based in New York City at that time). Little did I know that this moment in time would open a door for me to learn something that would take me on an incredible journey for the rest of my life. Since then, the music of the djembe has given me a language that allows me to communicate with people around the world. My heart is open and my soul is full of joy when I play these rhythms. I want to share these rhythms with you so you can speak with your heart by learning the language of this drum from the rhythms in this book.

How To Use This Book: This book is designed for the hand-drumming beginner who is interested in learning about traditional African rhythms and the standard practice of learning djembe or any hand drum. It is my hope that this book functions as a gateway to opening up your imagination while experimenting with the many different sounds, rhythms and techniques that are introduced in this book and DVD. Please keep in mind that much of Africa's history has been passed down orally from family to family, village to village, and there are many stories that describe the rhythms and dances. These rhythms will hopefully inspire you to explore African music and culture in its many forms as well as other percussion cultures from around the world. All of these rhythms can be applied, altered, and developed to fit your musical needs. Explore, experiment, and enjoy!

History of
The DJEMBE

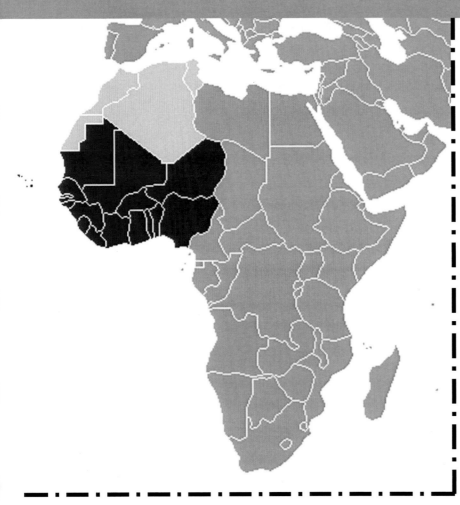

Djembe (pronounced JEM-bay) (also spelled as djimbe, jembe, jenbe, or yembe) is a skin-covered hand drum shaped like a large goblet and is played with bare hands. It is a member of the membranophone family of musical instruments. The djembe originated in West Africa, where it became an integral part of the area's music and tradition. As a result of the goblet shape, the density of the wood, the internal carvings, and the skin, there is a wide range of tones that can be produced by the djembe. The rounded shape with the extended tube of the djembe body gives it its deep bass and rich tone notes.

The primary tones of the djembe are generally referred to as "bass," "tone," and "slap." Striking the skin near the center with the palm produces a bass note; striking the skin nearer the rim with the fingers flat produces a tone, and the same position with the fingers relaxed so that the fingertips snap to the head of the drum produces a slap. The slap has a high, sharp sound and the tone is more round and full. Other notes exist, but only advanced drummers can consistently create sound distinct from the others.

The djembe drum is found in all of West Africa, where it is one of the most common instruments, but since the 1990s you can find djembes all over the continent. The origin of the djembe is associated with a class of Mandinka/Susu blacksmiths known as Numu. The wide dispersion of the djembe drums throughout West Africa may be due to Numu migrations dating from the first millennium A.D. Despite the associations of the djembe with the Numu, there do not appear to be hereditary restrictions upon who can play the djembe as occurs with some other African instruments.

The djembe first made an impact outside West Africa in Paris of the 1940s (and more widely in the 1950s), and in New York at the Worlds Fair in the 1960s, with Les Ballets Africains featuring a young Papa Ladji Camara on djembe, directed by Fodeba Keita of Guinea. This resulted in a surge of interest in African drumming, especially djembe drumming.

The djembe is said to contain three spirits: the spirit of the tree, the spirit of the animal of which the drum head is made, and the spirit of the instrument maker. Properly-crafted djembe drums are carved in one single piece from hollowed-out trees. Properly-made drums are not smooth on the interior but have a series of teardrop shaped divots inside that enhances the tonal qualities. In earlier times (and still in some rural areas) djembe were used to send messages over long distances.

(Adapted from http://en.wikipedia.org/wiki/Djembe)

Types of Tuning

Mechanically tuned djembes are tuned with a wrench in quarter- or half-turn increments. If your drum head is loose and you need to make it tighter, start by turning the nut counterclockwise, tightening each a quarter turn. Or, tighten one nut, then go to the opposite nut on the other side of the drum head. After that one, tighten the next nut moving in one direction around the head until you have tightened each nut a quarter turn. Repeat until the drum sounds good and tight as you like. Press in the center of the drum head. If there is a slight give to it, then you have room to continue tightening, or you can stop. Don't tighten too much or the skin may rip. You can loosen or tighten the nuts to make the bass of the drum sound lower or the tone and slap of the drum sound higher. Experiment.

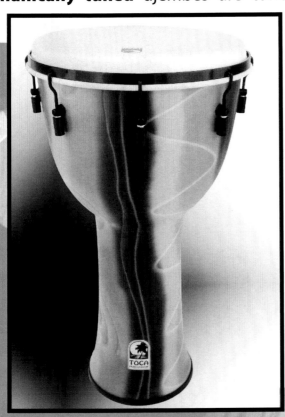

Rope tuned djembes use rope to tune the pitch of the drum head. An intricate weaving of rope is laced up and down the drum through rope hoops attached to a metal ring at the edge of the drum head and at the neck located just below the bowl. The ring system holds the skin in place and pulling the rope as tight as you can stretches the skin taunt. This is one of the traditional methods that evolved in the latter part of the 20th century. Prior to that drums were tightened with animal gut and pegs. Fire was used to draw out the moisture and tighten the skin. Electric hot plates were used not so long ago to do the same, but now djembe makers have designed tools to help pull the rope extremely tight.

Parts of the Djembe

Head: also known as the playing surface or skin of the djembe.

Bowl: the hollowed-out part of the instrument where the sound resonates.

Tail: the hollowed extension where the sound flows from.

Parts of the Djembe - Sizes

Traditionally, djembe drums are about 12" (30cm) in diameter, varying an inch or two, but can be found in sizes from 5" (13cm) up to 18" (46cm).

Most djembes from Mali, Guinea, Burkina Faso, and Senegal are still hand-carved from traditional species of wood, using traditional tools and methods. In the 1990s, djembes started being produced elsewhere, such as in Ghana, Nigeria, South Africa and Bali, often using modern machinery and substitute species of wood. However, these woods are softer and less dense than the traditional woods such as *lenke*, *djalla*, *dugura*, *gueni*, *gele* and *iroko*.

Holding the Drum

Holding the Drum - Part 1

There are two ways of holding the djembe. One is standing with the instrument strapped onto you and the second way is sitting in a chair. We are going to focus on sitting down in a chair.

First, place the djembe on the floor and pull it into the center of your body. You should sit up straight and close to the edge of the chair for optimum performance.

Second, tilt the drum forward at an angle away from your body. The drum sits gently between your knees and thighs.

Holding the Drum - Part 3

Third, place the heel of your left or right foot in front of the drum's tail at the bottom of the drum.

The front foot should have a slight outward angle that is comfortable with your foot flat on the floor.

Holding the Drum - Part 4

Fourth, place your left or right foot at the back of the drum's tail.

Holding the Drum - Part 5

Fifth, the drum needs air to vibrate, so you must maintain the tilted position to allow air to come through the bottom of the drum's tail.

Hand Positions

Place both hands in the center of the djembe making the shape of a triangle. Touch your index fingers together at their tips and your thumbs should face and touch each other. Be sure to close all of your fingers as best as you can. This will help you produce a full tone and bass sound.

Three Sounds of the Djembe

Bass

Play with a relaxed, flat hand. Play slightly off-center for best sound quality. Keep the triangle position. Pull the sound out of the drum.

Tone

Play with a relaxed, flat hand, keeping your fingers closed. Hit the drum like you're hitting a nail with a hammer. Keep the triangle position. Pull the sound out of the drum.

Slap

Play with a relaxed, curved hand, keeping your fingers slightly apart. The tips of your fingers strike the surface, making the high pitched slap sound.

 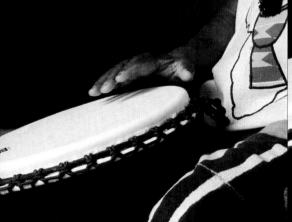 

Overview of Playing Technique

The following photos show the basic technique in which your hand strikes the head of the djembe. Refer to the DVD for more information.

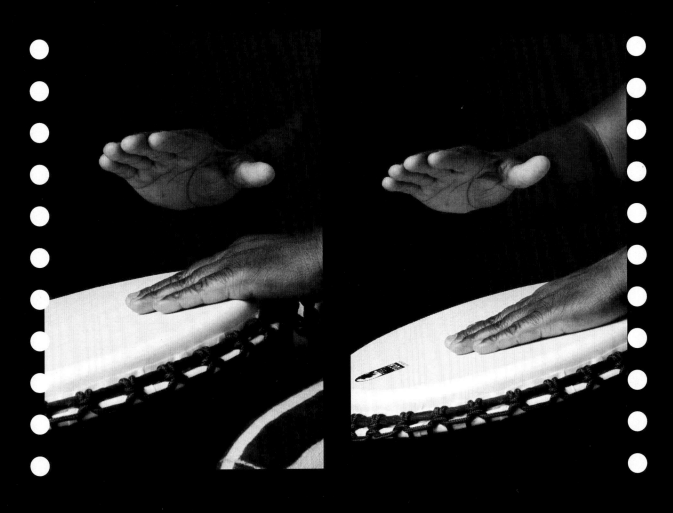

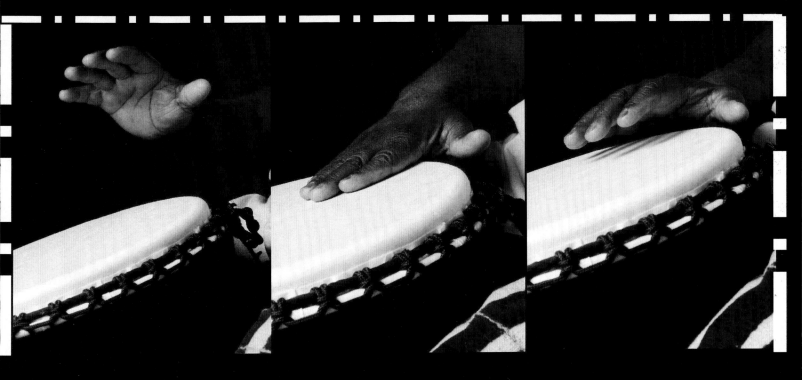

Other Techniques

(Harmonic) Finger Touch: This is a finger technique used on the

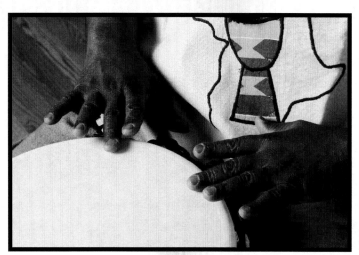

edge of the drum. The natural harmonics of the drum ring with a bell-like quality giving you another musical sound option from the djembe. Play any combination of rhythms you choose.

Muted Finger Roll: This technique is played rapidly like an open-

handed roll or a single-stroke roll as used on a snare drum. The roll is muted because the player is pushing into the head of the drum which bends the pitch and stops the drum from ringing.

Harmonic Overtone Fingering: Place your middle finger on the center of the drum head and hit the edge of the drum head with your other hand. If done correctly, you should hear a bell-pitch ring, which is one of the overtones

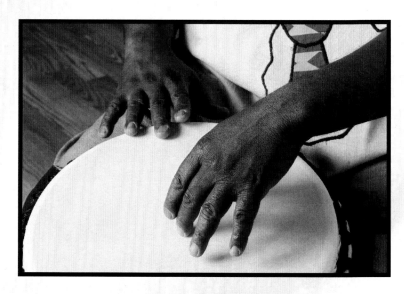

of the djembe. Experiment to find other overtones.

Traditional Djembe Rhythms

Demonstrated Djembe Rhythms

Drum Notation

Note: if you don't read music, no problem! All the rhythms are clearly demonstrated on the DVD. Use the "chapter selections" menu on the DVD to find the rhythm you want to work on, and learn by copying what is played. Then, look at the corresponding page in the book and you will see how the rhythm looks on paper!

B - Bass

T - Tone

S - Slap

OS - Open Slap

CS - Closed Slap

Tch - Touch

M - Mute

MS - Muted Slap

PR - Palm Roll

FR - Finger Roll

DE - Drum Edge

R - Right Hand

L - Left Hand

LAMBAN

pronounced Lahm-ba

Break / Cue

Rhythm 1

Rhythm 2

LAMBAN

Gallop Rhythm

Bass Rhythm

SUNU

pronounced Su Nu

Break / Cue

T S S T S S S T T T   T S   T T T

 = **Flam** - two notes played at the same time - one hitting the drum head before the other.

Ghost Notes - hand and fingers touching the skin lightly.

SUNU

Rhythm 1

Rhythm 2

Rhythm 3

MANDIANI

pronounced   Mendiani / Manjani

Break / Cue

MANDIANI

Rhythm 1

accompaniment rhythm - triplet feel

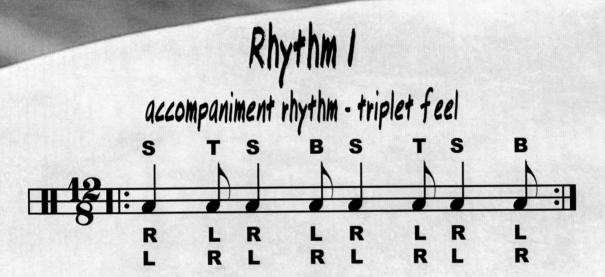

Rhythm 2

accompaniment rhythm - slap tone slap (wait)

with/o bass note

Rhythm 2

accompaniment rhythm - Billy Bongo

GOUMBÉ

Break / Cue

Rhythm 1
with doubled hand pattern

Rhythm 2
ghost notes help with the timing of this rhythm

ZAOULI

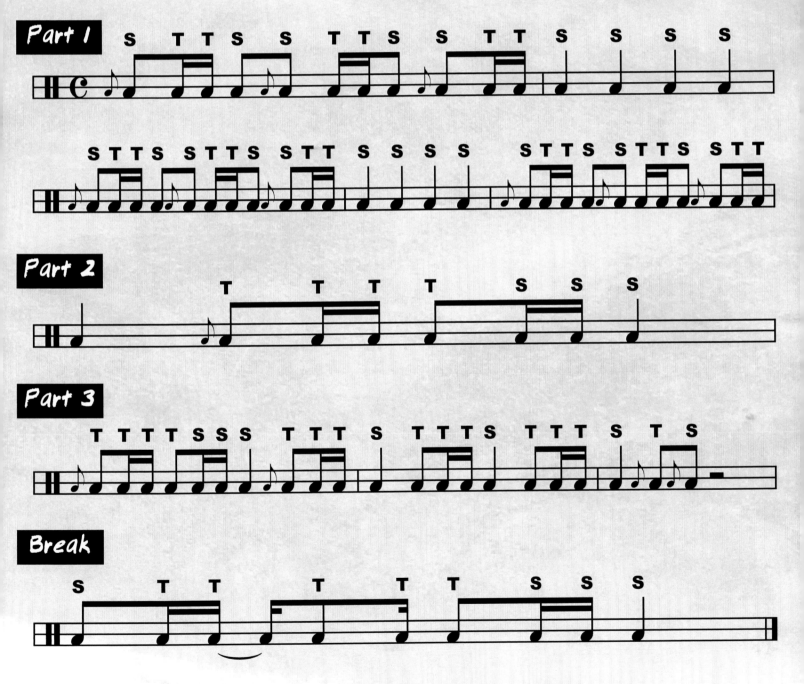

Part 1

Part 2

Part 3

Break

KUKU

Break / Cue

Rhythm 1

Rhythm 2

KU KU FOR CO CO PUFFS KU KU FOR CO CO PUFFS

RHYTHM	ETHNIC GROUP	REGION
LAMBAN	MANDE	GUINEA
SUNU	KASSOUNKÉ	MALI
MANDIANI	MALINKE	GUINEA
GOUMBÉ	AKAN	GHANA
ZAOULI	GOURO	IVORY COAST
KUKU	MANIAN	IVORY COAST

Michael Wimberly Discography (playing djembe and percussion)

Album/Song	Label	Artist
Drop Kick	RCA/Novus	Steve Coleman & 5 Elements
Def Trance Beat	RCA/Novus	Steve Coleman & 5 Elements
Tales of Three Cities	RCA/Novus	Steve Coleman & 5 Elements
Anthems	Living Music	Paul Winter Consort
Angel on a Stone Wall	Living Music	Paul Halley
Cruisin" (single)	EMI	D'Angelo
Speaking the Mamma Tongue	Raven Records	John McDowell
Coming Home	Independent	Mamma Tongue
Rock the Cathartic Spirit	Koch International	Jean Paul Bourelly
Digital Griot (CD-ROM)	LTI/Voyager	Betty Saar
Gioia 2	ital Records, Inc.	Lives of a Cell
Deconstruction Reconstruction	Ear Light	Michael Wimberly
At the Center of the Threshold	Ear Light	Positive Knowledge

www.powerofdrum.com

Ear Light Music is a MW Productions Sound Design record label.

Recommended Listening:
Frere Coulibaly
M'Bemba Bangoura
Fanta Kouyate
Famoudou Konate
Mamady Keita
Kalani
Magbana

Acknowledgments: Anthony Citrinite and Tony Maggiolino at The Collective; Memo Acevedo, Victor Filonovich, Steve Nigohosian, Jeff Ivester, Terry Tlatelpa, and Sergio Bonsignore at TOCA Percussion; Steven M. Lobmeier at Evans/D'Addario; Aldo Mazza and Dr. Jolan Kovacs-Mazza at KOSA, JazzAzores; Together with Music; Craig Brown; George Kiteley; Raymond A. Graham; Abu Shabazz; Kweyao Agypon; Ladji Camera; James Cherry; Jalal Sharieff; Rudy Walker; Bradley Simmons; Abdel Salaam; Chuck Davis; Hank Johnson; Ronnie Roc; Janice Zelesky; Margot Faught; Alice Teirstein; Nia Love-Roney; Paul Winter; Dyane Harvey-Salaam; Jewel Kinch; Dana Elquist; Forces of Nature Dance Theatre; Alvin Ailey American Dance Theatre; Urban Bush Women; National Song and Dance Co. of Mozambiqe; Joan Millers Dance Players; Complexions Dance Co.; Ethical Culture Fieldston School; NYC Department of Education; NYC Museum for African Art; Arts Connection; Summer Arts Institute; Power of Drum.